The View from the Crowd

Ebony Hogan

Presentation by *BookLeaf Publishing*

Web: www.bookleafpub.com

E-mail: info@bookleafpub.com

ISBN: 9789358317428

First edition 2024

For my dad

Who taught me how to love music

(even if he doesn't like most of the artists in here)

ACKNOWLEDGEMENT

Perfect people come in threes and I wouldn't
have written this without
Mum, dad, Levi
My wonderful niece, nephew, and dog
Holly, Emily, Fiachra

You make me write and I wouldn't be me
without you.

Additional thanks to all the people who make
concerts happen. This book wouldn't exist
without you.
And of course to all the musicians who inspired
my writing:
The Fillers
The Bootleg Beatles (and the originals- of
course)
Mumford and Sons
Bon Jovi
Hozier
Dodie
Amigo the Devil
Bastille
Florence and the Machine
Panic! At the Disco

Rainbow Kitten Surprise
The Killers
and The Amazing Devil

To experience these artists the way I do, find my
playlist 'The View from the Crowd' on Spotify
https://open.spotify.com/playlist/46oLRsEOuqjL
tChjriAwoG?si=bc498e2b87264463

15/07/2014

I've been here many times before.
I grew up on these shores,
playing in these waters,
climbing this cohort of sand and stone.

The start isn't of interest
so we waste away at the strand.
Skimming stones, sharing stories,
singing along with Skulls 'N' Roses.
Until the end of the set calls to us and we ascend.

Seven familiar notes start to play.
F-D-F-D-E-D-F
The dance begins.
The first of many times
where I'm swarmed,
swallowed,
pressured from all sides with waves
of love for the notes being played-
and the people playing them.

It's not the real thing.
The real thing is miles away, in precious LA
but we scream along anyway,
indifferent to everything that isn't this.

I'm coming out of my childhood
and I'm doing just fine.

Warm-Up

Standing, shivering impatiently.
Left to wait, bodies pressed against bodies
in a way that nobody ever wants to be.
Just as you're thinking
this is the worst part of the process.
Is it even worth it if I have to do this?
Lights go down. A false start- we stall,
cheering rises, and then fades.
Lights turn back on and it's not what we want.
Gawky, awkward, inexperienced.
Ancient, washed out, fame adjacent.
The people no one comes to see beside
the smattering of fans at the back of the hall.
Between songs, they give their social media,
requests of merchandise purchases.
They're begging people to sing along.

Sometimes they're worse than the shivering.
Sometimes they're skilled
Always, they're there.
Warming us up until ticket promises are
fulfilled.

28/10/2018

Five minutes before they come on,
you tell me about someone
who knows someone
who knew someone
who knows you.
The first someone is famous
but I've already forgot them.

I'm watching the elderly man at the front.
He dances with his whole being,
throwing himself at the music
like this performance is just for him.
I wonder if he danced like this
to the real thing
in the sixties.

You complain about the person
down the row
clapping out of time.
Off-
Beat.
Each time we clap, their foot taps
a second later. Driving you silently mad.

On stage, the band flows through the eras.

Bowl-cut black and white,
four different coloured suits,
multi-coloured icons.
We travel through time with them
while they play the music we both grew up with
thirty years apart.

27/11/2018

5

The beat is the first thing I notice.
It hits hard; heavy and consistent-
pounding my eardrums.
They sing about death and but it's gentle.

The idea of somebody departing softly-
with a whimper. Without pain.
The melody fights with the rhythm to be heard
they layer over one another with the voice of a
stadium
coming out on top
and suddenly

the instruments are in sync in a way I've never
heard before.
Folk/Rock/Country/Music -
Stamping feet and raised arms
in time with banjo strings and bass drums.
I wouldn't have it any other way.

16/6/2019

He stands centre stage.
Tall,
experienced,
proud,
like he was born to be here.
It starts to rain and he declares,
the angels are crying.
Before me is a man with confidence unmatched.

But I'm here with you not him.
I watch the thrill buzz through you-
feeling pride that you want me here, fear that
you don't.
Once you're on your feet nothing can move you
except the beat which jolts your body.
It's built into your being.
A rhythm your heart has beat to since you were
my age.
A rhythm that flows through the veins of your
friends
niece
sister
children
and one day your grandchildren too.

When I was young you played this music so
loud it hurt my ears.
Here I sing with the force of the crowd.
With the force that you taught me.

The drive home is
long
quiet
dark
exhausting
but I'm here with you.

27/06/2019

The bars in front of me,
hot to the touch from the sun.
It beats down as if knowing
I've been waiting for this day for months.

Usually the antics around interest me most
but today I only see him in all his long-haired
glory.
Talented fingers and beautiful voice.
I follow every note he plays.

Baby. Honey. Love. Darling.
We scream louder with each term of endearment,
with each expression of longing.
He sings sweet nothings into the machine
and we churn them back with affectionate
aggression.

The screen behind him turns black. Then grey.
Grey shirts of those who fight.
Rainbow coloured marches.
Green-tinted hateful oppressors.
Red blood of those being oppressed.

Through it all he sings.

Love. Joy. Sweetness. Sex.
The crowd melts
under the heat of the sun.
It beats down as if knowing he's on stage.

You are in the Earth of Me

I walk down the street alone, between houses, up
hidden steps.
Alone, I open the door and sit on the table
and make what I want known.
She takes the needle, kisses my skin,
and starts to carve your music.

Only a six month relationship,
but I'm ready to have you forever.
To hold you in the earth of me
and in turn you'll remind me to be -
brave,
bold,
strong,
with your epitaph I love so much.

The carving is done and that night
I scream your words and hear them whispered
back.
They bounce off the cubicle walls.
Scalding hot water slips down the drain,
salty from tears.
Rivulets of red
drip down my skin,
as my body bleeds to make room for you.

Your words were there
when I needed them to be.
When words of my own weren't enough.
I wrote them into my notebook,
taking them into myself
and churning back art.
Alone.

19/09/2021

Queued in shivering cold
we walk a mile
buy some wine
shuffle back down the line.
Have our tickets scanned,
find a place to stand
holding drinks in hand
throw them carelessly down our throats.
Feelings of bliss trickle down slowly.
Do I belong here?

The stage glows – R O Y G B P
Colours of ourselves
we glow too – flushed red from alcohol
I can never tell if I belong.

Apples and Peaches,
Pelicans and oboes.
Beds and bra straps and the beauty in you
that I see. That I forget-
How could I forget?
The song about Him.
The song about *Him*.
The song about us that I'd never admit to.
Your breath is warm on my skin.
I don't think I belong.

01/04/2022

We took a train to Manchester, me and this
stranger.
Navigating streets we've never seen before.
Getting in the door without being ID'd,
the cider I buy fits in the pockets of my men's
jeans.
Barely six metres away, the stage stands short.
And when he comes on it's like he's in the
crowd.
A wave, an American accent, a banjo in hand.
No talking before he starts to pick at the strings;
smacking them, slapping them, his voice filling
the small room.
We move together in response, the waves of
drug abuse
and murder bounce across the crowd.
I look to the stranger who'd had no idea what to
expect.
It wasn't this. Cocaine. Bingo. Quick tempo.
Stories being built before our eyes.
He stops singing to speak and for once we speak
back.
What's usually a one sided conversation
has turned into group contribution.

He speaks of his dog and his journey and his
songs.
He apologises to the strangers we dragged along.
He promises we're not a cult but I'm not so sure.
The sense of community is stronger than ever
before.
The group is small but we make it feel large;
the love in the room stands strong.
We're all here for a reason.
Listening to these fucked up songs:
we can relate to the pain and the sorrow
and the anger that he sings about in such a gentle
way.
Our lullabys rock the room and we
metaphorically hold hands.
We pull each other through the sounds of
suffering.

08/04/2022

The couple beside me are antithetical.
One bright and blooming. Blue hair and warm
eyes,
he sidesteps so he doesn't block my view.
The other stands behind him, arms folded; dark
and brooding.
A protective shadow that I can't help but adore.

We crouch together, as one. Twenty thousand
people. Forty thousand
bent knees. Forty thousand eyes on the man
ahead.
A phone, fallen to the floor.
Their life abandoned in a moment of joy.
We give it to the bright man, who passes it on to
the shadow, beaming.

Forty thousand knees straightened, twenty
thousand voices
together, as one. We jump out of time but
grinning and singing, together, as one.

Ob La Di

When did I first learn to love music? Was it the
lullabies sang to me?
Was it the pop-party fuelled discos? Was it
dancing to random CDs
- alone in my room that smelled of paint and
childhood?

The actual answer is obvious honestly.
I would be sat in the old office chair-
the one with a hole in the leather.
You would turn on the speakers
and spread your folders across the desktop.

You taught me about The Jam,
Queen, The Who, Pink Floyd,
Blondie, Chumbawamba,
and, of course, the ones to avoid.

The most important of all, we listened to them
often.
Playing the tunes from the 60s,
basking in the 70s
mourning in the 80s.
It would be a long time before I understood
the meaning behind the words you belt

but for now we dive side-by-side
in a yellow submarine,
drifting past the octopus' garden,
getting by with a little help…

We sing about Desmond together-
your voice drowning out mine in a way that I
adore.
One day my voice will drown out his
and the three of us will sing an encore.

Ob La Di,
Ob La Da,
La La how life goes on…

Ob La Da

Ten tiny fingers...
Chubby cheeks and thighs.
An angelic face when he's sleeping,
when we're alone, mischief in his eyes.
What wouldn't I do for you?

When I'm first left with him for any length of
time
he misses his mama and starts to cry.
I'm desperate to give her some downtime,
so I bounce and spin and shake a variety,
of blue-coloured animals in his eyeline.

Eventually, there's nothing left to do but sing
(sing!)

I haven't been to all the baby groups,
I don't know the rhymes.
But I know what was sang to me
so we sway to an upbeat-beat and I mime.
Too shy, even around him, to find the words
but they'll come – in time.

(A year to the day, phone balanced behind my
knee, hidden just enough so he wont see as it
makes a record of his life.

Me: *What are you singing?*
He screeches in response, lost in the tune.
Me: *Are you singing..?* Before I can finish...
Him: *YEAH yeah yeah yeah*
We look at each other. I see so much in you.
So small and yet you changed everything
Us:
Ob la di
Oh da da
Lala how life goes on...)

03/02/2023

You've been incredible, Manchester.
She looks angelic, stage lighting making her dress
shine.
I just need one more thing from you tonight,
The crowd shouts and surges forwards, willing to
give
their lives for this queen of songs and sin and
substance abuse.
We know what's coming- *we raise it up, this offering.*

The person in front of me turns and for once I don't
overthink-
I grab someone's hand and she puts her shoulders
beneath my knees.
I'm finally pulling my head above water.
The view from up here is breathtaking-
the bobbing heads of thousands of fans
crowding around my waist.

The stage is gloriously uninterrupted
and I get to watch- transfixed- as the angel
removes her floral halo and offers it to the crowd,
sacrificing her gift, gifting it to us.
I raise my arms and she turns me to gold in the
stagelight.

10/03/2023

Eyeliner.
Black shirt.
Alcohol.
You.
All I need.
To get me through

We drink. Climb the steps.
I've never been this high before.
The stage is in the distance. Almost out of
sight of my black-ringed eyes.
Your hand is on mine as the music starts.
We could be the only people here.
When I bought the tickets
I didn't know this would be his last.
But here we are, on the precipice of history.
Me and you.
Lights flash violently.
The music I've been listening to
since I was twelve.
Since the day I met you-
What a beautiful wedding.

(When I was twelve you got me through.
When you were twelve, I got you through.

A friendship that lasts the lifespan of a band.
I hold your hand while you walk through hell.
My grip slips but you never seem to notice.
We'll keep on getting each other through.)

29/03/2023

Five-two isn't the ideal height for this kind of place.
My toes always hurt as much as my throat,
both straining to be on the same level as everybody
else.
Today we've found a spot that's almost perfect. I
can't see
the piano, but I see Ela's face.
That's the important part.

I'm transfixed by her make-up. The crowd is full of
put together people,
trying to impress perfect strangers.
Ela doesn't give a shit.
Lipstick smeared across her face, matching
clown-like eyeliner.
She spins, ill-fitting dress flying out around her,
hair in scattered patches from male pattern baldness
and the depression she sings so passionately about.

We chant for her biggest song during the encore.
She's left us waiting.
"You've guessed it!" Ela yells.
We all scream in response and then fall in sync to
sing about Satan.

Nowhere

There is no other feeling like
the feeling of unwavering solidarity.
When I'm here, I'm not alone. I can look back
months later and know that I'm never alone.

There is no way I'd rather spend my time
than on the train, car, bus then
standing waiting around for hours, feet sore
and back aching, until the stage is filled.

There is no sound I'd rather hear
than the agonising pounding
of the twelve-foot speakers.
They tower above and inflict pain
and endless love.

There is no way I'd rather spend
the pounds and pennies I scrape together.
Every birthday and Christmas used
for these few hours of unmatched indulgence.

There is nowhere else in the world
where I'm more at home than here.
Surrounded by you, by people,
who love what I love.
Surrounded by music.

Every gig I go to leaves me a little more in love than
before.

02/07/2023

We're surrounded by walls built by the Romans.
Made of arches standing strong.
They hold onto one another with immovable
grace.
A balcony stretches above each arc- framing the
top of the walls
with metal that bends like the branches of a tree.
Most of the crowd stands crowded
within the ground protected by walls.
But some people are scattered on the balcony-
watching from afar.

I wonder who they are and how they got there.
Shop owners, musical family,
high up producers, and close friends
are all possibilities.

A couple stands together,
with only inches between them.
I watch them as they prepare for the show.
They shuffle around one another to find the best
spots.
One of them has a walking stick,
(a possible reason for their presence on the
balcony)

The branch gets left behind,
soft hand clinging onto soft hand instead.
When the arches finally echo sounds of joy,
their hands raise together – fingers interlaced-
clasped tightly.

Two fists together,
united with the bliss of music.

13/07/2023

27

Standing behind that person who
skipped 42 places in the queue
to press against the barrier beside the stage.
Anger starts to flow, I watch the singer's rage.
He waves to the side, showing obvious pain
from his overworked load leaving him drained.

I'm drained by how the crowd
pushes in waves, beating me, drowning me.
Sometimes we're together, as one.
Today I'm falling apart. Alone.
Waited for hours but now I'm done.

Sounds of the Night

I push my headphones
into my phone's headphone jack,
place the buds in my ears
and listen...

The music starts to flow,
vibrations pushing their way through metal and
plastic,
to tap a rhythm upon my skin,
to raise the hair on my arms and
make my heart forget to beat.

I close my eyes, allowing the darkness to
swallow me
until all there is is music.
It echoes, bounces, pushes into my being
like the roots of a tree planting themselves.
Unyielding.
When I breathe, the cold air hits my lungs.
When they sing, their breath copies mine.
My lips imitate, until the chorus comes
and we become one.

Each muscle, each nerve, each cell
feels the enticing flow

of the indescribable music,
that fuels my self
that allows me
to continue
living.

I carry your logo on my chest

At each and every gig I attend,
as a record of all the concerts.
I make my way to the merch stand
and buy myself a brand new t shirt.

I empty my pockets and fork out the money
for something I don't really need.
Extortionate prices most of the time
but it's worth it for my new short sleeve.

I don't know why I do it,
but by now I've come too far
I have to get a new t shirt
instead of going to the festival bar.

And now every day before I go out
all I think about as I get dressed
is how people will see me and know who I love-
because I carry your logo on my chest.

01/09/2023

The real thing. The one and only.
We stand in the mushy ground,
melted away by Ireland's endless rain.
We sink and shuffle and sigh until
there they are.
Like they knew I was here nine years ago.

Drums, strings, voice upon voice
upon thousands of voices.
Arms in the air, feet beating the grass down.
The experience of the band is reflected
in the adoration of the crowd.
Forty thousand and five people
making this moment perfect.

As the bass pounds heavy,
and the drums take over-
(the drummer directing the crowd like
we're just another instrument he's playing)
I think about the night nine years ago
at that cohort of sand and stone.

I'm coming into my adulthood
and I'm doing just fine.